Graveyard Dogs

Graveyard Dogs

Poems by

Jason Brightwell

Cover design by Jason Brightwell
Author's photograph by Chelsea Raithby

ISBN: 978-1-63980-377-4

Kelsay Books
502 South 1040 East, A-119
American Fork, Utah 84003
Kelsaybooks.com

for Gina and Rick,
Phyllis, Amiel,
and Erin

Acknowledgments

The author would like to thank the editors at the following journals where some of these poems were previously published:

Book of Matches Journal: "At Café Black," "Rust"
Buried Letter Press: "Graveyard Dogs," "The Big Catch"
Cacti Fur Magazine: "Nighttime in the ICU"
East Coast Literary Review: "Grounding," "Resting Easy"
Gravel Magazine: "Sea Legs"
Metaworker Magazine: "Beautiful Grief," "Last Meal"
Ocotillo Review: "One of Us is Dead"
The Orchards Poetry Review: "Comfort Remains," "Family History the Hard Way"
Right Hand Pointing Magazine: "Times of Need"
Sky Island Journal: "Blood Clot"
Straightforward Poetry Review: "Psalms"
Vending Machine Press: "Rainy Season"

Contents

I

One of Us Is Dead

One of Us is Dead

but late some nights,
drunk in dancing
vices, I can't

distinguish which.
In those poorly
drawn hours, we

are only shaky
tracings of what
we were. Fine

lines blur. Mine
bind me, engraved
to earth, yours

climb upward, and
shine, carving your
name across the sky.

Night Gardening

An odd time for coral
bells, green-edged,
purple—varicose swell.

While dark mother
swaddles her unnaturals
under gash in sky,

you've passed yard's far
edge, where fences bend
toward world's end.

How odd it is to say
where in the world, knowing
not where nowhere is.

Times of Need

Under blanket, earth worm, bedpan
cringe, nurses change shifts, leave
your memory at the door.

You are there but not as much, naked
tree, dying battery, respirator.

Show me your age, hand over loss,
time is full of lost seconds and you are
craving.

Leaves fall. Wash them from you,
lazy drinker, scrub the skin clean,
muscle up,

bleed it out in drunken ribbons,
expose the bone.
Try to catch what you have done.

Rust

I've seen older,
but the truck was
old. Old enough for
thin skin. Skin

pitted with black
nightmares, worn
through. Sharp in flake
and auburn lumps. What

weakness makes
it choose to choose.
Some soft spot, a pinprick,
a funeral home.

Supernovae Folk Explosion

Night sky is silver flash
with hammers and nails
but starless—

a folk explosion and nothing.
Luminous. Gone.
I am free, supernovae,
an orphan at last.

Particles, waves. Progenitors,
your sighing is my ancestry.
You mattered.

I keep my rooms tidy.
They heave with you.

We can't hear your voices
squeezing. We don't listen
to the rain coming
from the astral side
of wind—some

other country where bonds
stronger than death fade into
dark like dead galaxies,
like you.

Rainy Season

Drizzle is a morning
blanket under where we orphan
birds are lulled to quiet still.

On drier days, predawn rose
in trumpet notes, its first pink
hints tinging the corners of night.

But damp tension hangs on
the curtain of early day—
a low growl, concerning gray.

Until it passes, rumbling
intentions, we hold on, tombstone
tight, for fear of toppling
into life.

Between Funerals

Quiet out now, only low
hum. Slow oaken split,
satin bleed.

Plump workers, fertile
ground. Drool in root
web, under-sludge.

Markers seem silly
from here. Waxy heads,
graveyard teeth. We all

laugh in dirt between
funerals. Best to take
the toothache home.

Chemo (Enough Already)

Even hunger has
left her. Ill evening
hours take

toll, dry heaving
through the night.
Light finds her

exhausted. Ginger
ale lunch, chipped
ice dinner. Sick

again soon. No real
point in meals now,
the grave on her

mind keeps her
full and ill
enough already.

Rise and Shine

Wake up, you failed
promise of man, it's time
to shine your light

is out and you are worthless,
alone in your body
no single hope to float my

next moments will be far
different from yours just because

the sun is out does
not mean you are ok.

Keep falling, save restraint
for fools. Make do with
your phantom heart

ache in private like the rest
of us. Teach your tongue
to die laughing at

old wounds occupy space in
your head with alcohol, loss
and whatever

you do just please don't listen
when I tell you how much
I miss you.

Intensive Care

for Amiel

arcadian night
faint murmur
energy muster
finger flutter
preflight angel

nearby dozing,
holding space-
heavyhearted guardian
instantly there
to sooth and offer
tender whispers.
Soft beeps.
Tiny lights.

Blood Clot

Dark between two falling stars
it won't have to travel far.

Arching low—earthen flung
a crooked bow towards the ground,

tainted veins, earthworm swell, floods
bloat, push the dead back out.

I wondered aloud, there wandering,
eternal damp, lost patch of dark,

how it is that nostalgia rubs
rough memories smooth.

Instead, I learned to close my eyes,
to see invisible breezes

heavy with storm warnings—
warm and low and ominous

as the day your veins delivered
that bitter gift to your own heart.

Orchid

Thin of stalk and frail.
Nodes like knuckles,
arthritic.

Roots shrink—shed
hair. You stopped
taking water.

Still, blossoms pale,
bleached, nod
toward memory,

in new bloom despite
the tar you found
yourself transplanted.

Everything Matters

Unpack your dead
under star
less night.

Let them shine,
finally, if only in
your eye.

Inflate a flat heart,
rough lips. Relax.

Stretch them out. Remember.
Then burn them.

There is nothing
more than
this.

Be stronger. Dissect your
own night
mares.

Write a word
less eulogy. Come to
terms.

Set your bones in
the breathless gap between
end and

start of that one looping
memory you will
never shake.

Painting Graves

Once you were purple-
rich, aqua deep, vibrant—
kaleidoscope.

We were mute, wire lipped,
fish-eyed shock,
when yellow foamed
at your soul.

None of us will survive this.
You were first, seams
bleeding.

And because grief falls into
itself, I am the dull
grey of a tombstone in drizzle.

Unable to see any silver in the
sky beyond this jet black
of funerals.

Ramshackle

When you come
from where you went, will
you quiet my eyes so I
can see as you?

Shut them, curious things.
Bring me, at last, black,
so sightless, clear.

You are a collection of
reverence, razor
blades, rust and blood.

Content to linger, I
imagine your soft invisibility,
peace, but are you coming

back from black?

We can vibrate together,
sharp and strained,
a family of lost sounds,
reunited, moving on.

Satellite

I could see there was nothing, blind
eye—feral, free, you liquor-
breathing drunk.

I'd been near—ready, vices
steering, but this was closer
to death.

You orbited it—yellow as a tired
moon. Lost in old wounds, too
low to even die.

Razor sick shadow back,
how fast you showed me
giving up.

Long gone,
trip on a devil's tale—
hush at last, flatline lips.

Not much for me—
lost dog, head tilt, I don't
recognize names

but I can still starve on
the familiar shards
of your shattered heart.

II

Beautiful Grief

Force Feed

Full belly
ache of funerals,
pregnant with lilies,
praying night-

mares. If weaker,
I'd have begged—
a wretch in winter,
for mercy.

But I have given up
my grief to ground's
mouth. Shoved it in,
til green-

lipped and filled,
a field of fed
mouths—slit silent,
thinking mercy.

At Cafe Black

A diet of funerals—
sour tooth
raw tongue.

Dark waitress
lean, slick—drains
her pot, takes
measurements.

She's in the kitchen
hot plate
embalming table,

whispering,
horned cook,
their grins crack—
fissure in bone.

They fill me up—
burned heart,
stomachache.

Time to go. She jots
my epitaph,
hands me the grave.

Comforter

Dad died with vodka
labels tattooed on his palms.
When I found him, he was
the color of drywall,
wrapped in a blanket.
He'd been treating his gout
alone
dingy mummy wraps
held his digits on.
I can picture him shambling
into death drunk, my
Dad, more scabs than skin,
asking directions
to a wedding
between dread and joy,
Unable to speak his sadness
in life, he left for me a language
of guilt in dried blood,
brown as the blanket he leaned into
for comfort.

Siamese

Dear brother, bare reflection,
naked in my eye, a mirror is our
maker.

We move in unison,
silent silver. Before I leave,
let's find a fire, melt memory.

You don't really need me
anymore—I've eaten all the grief,

combed loss from your head,
scrubbed dead off your skin. So

tell me again how you'll read my
eulogy, long and slow—
a leaving train.

I want to embrace the empty
graves between the words
you will not use.

Beautiful Grief

You wore grey fate
perfectly—laughter,
golden touch. It was a show,

of course. Even as tiny
hope rippled over private
blue melancolia,

it stirred up sludge,
lingering at bottom's black—
terminal and terrible and certain.
You and I knew it.

We ached in private.
Mine, a pinwheel of gloom,
yours, somehow, a rainbow
of beautiful grief.

Loose Dirt

Cast me out,
empty eye. I see
what you are hiding.

Tell me first how heavy
your sickness is—
weight-split paper skin.

And what name you gave
the bottle god—this grief
has gotten dangerous.

Nap in loose dirt, graveyard
dog, dream of soft and
guiltless still. Don't

wake up. Out of time.
That plot is warm
and familiar
and not for us.

Luck

I wish they weren't
the last drops of scotch
spilling over bottle's edge—
malt drizzle and empty.

I'm the ex-ex-smoker, quitting
quitting, fingers drunk,
ashtray fumble—
cigarillo CPR.

I step on and crack the
sacrificial bowl I'd crafted
(tried everything to save you)
life abbreviates fast as

lost breath—
the EMT
the DNR
the RIP.

Galactic Graveyard

When even nothing
is empty and the full
moon is gnashing—

jackal-born, a bright
white agony, I can still pick the
biggest stars, the oldest,

long dead but dreaming,
their most vivid light not
even close.

I see your names,
dimly lit in that far off
afterglow of death.

Stars align—celestial epitaphs
light the sky so that my
gashed skin is gleaming,

and while I don't recall
my first memory, I will
gush about my last.

A Case for Leaving

Tired packed his bags
shoveled in a mouthful of coal,
burned his way through last week.

I keep going. Wheels, track-free,
spin further from a promise of sleep.

Dry rubbed eyes are gunpowder
black. The future is a misfire.

Delirium—my toothbrush twin,
we wear matching pajamas,

and laugh at how fatigue says
good morning.

Skintight, full.
I'm no longer alone in here.

My seams are not
as neat as they should be and

my presence is looking back from
a leaving train.

I lean in and
whisper to myself, funeral
numb, that tomorrow is

long gone
and I will never sleep again.

Last Meal

Tomorrow is too
late. I've been listening
to the ground lick its

lips, laying plans to close
on your heart. To beat
the earth, brown

batter, to bake a
funeral bread. To
leave me hungry.

Yet we eat. We eat
and weep and fill ourselves
with songs we sang

when we were young,
before we thought
these things, unthinkable.

Dog Talk

In the far sky she spied
stars, cockeyed.

Like her; end stage,
emitting crooked light

and away she went sailing.

Autumn crept in, a burnt
orange whisper, before I saw him

again, the color of a dog,
feral—frightened.

Alone, baring teeth, daring
death to drink him down.

Our broken language,
grew furious in its simplicity,

we heaved nonverbal
threats like sharpened pikes.

Guilt has many faces, these choose us.
We nose around floorboards for secrets,

muzzle up in the heavy heart of
an empty house,

drunkenly dream of stars
freshly straightened, wonder-eyed,

and secretly hope neither of us will be
here if we ever wake up.

Full on Empty

I'm sideways here
flat like a sinking sun—
pink wither and gone.

Sofa topography is
a new tattoo.

Auction myself to dust
and odd house noise.

Funny how empty looks
and smells the same.

floorboard foot tap
as you passed.

They creak now
in long slow sighs,
full of worry.

Orchid, Cont'd.

Take a breath.
These last years were
crooked. Over

now, just relax.
Your garden yearns
for you. See us.

Lean low, Orchid,
beneath your leaves,
soiled now, sure,

but feel how we root.
Figuring out which
ways to go.

Autopsy Jigsaw

He greyed in living heartache,
brittle aging paper mâché.

All he had left were drinking
games with death, who
made pocket space.

Dad drank till regret sweat out,
his tomorrows were burning.

Now here is me,
childhood free, invited into
a retiring room—

quiet as the hollow
chambers of a stopped heart.

I've caught him in repose,
child cheeks flush,
dreamy afterlife.

still, color and all, he is
ill fit—our dead are
a puzzle to solve,

but he does look happy,
small, swaddled in
his mortuary robes.

Family History the Hard Way

I am in the dark, apart.
Science class frog, poison
tongue.

Doomed Jack, drunk on
time, finding wrong ways to
die.

Hungover.

Morning's guarantee grabs
breakfast to go.

Last night's smashed plates
are chewing teeth.

I saw your cancer in a picture
from the early 80s. You were
weeding out flowers.

The pearls in your ears were
words you never put in mine.

Pin me back, butterfly,
all wings stop eventually.

My heart is racing
but not for you.

Water Skeleton

Soaked. Barley and
malt—rubber-boned.

At this point, 100 proof, I'd
take the beached-fish

route—let the gush of high
tide ride me far up shore

past my pulverized dead,
crushed in drunken froth,

broken to bits by the things
in their lives that kept them
wet and killed them,

so the glaring white sun
may pick my bones from the

wet womb of my own private
underworld, bleach them

back a constitution,
and dry them into being.

Tiny Deaths

Deep orange—90 tiny
suns, a month's supply,
three slow sunsets a day.

Gluttonous and stupid,
I cram suns, comets, fireballs
from the sky.

The next two dry weeks
between now and velveteen,
I'm poorly drawn—

shaky lines aching for just one
setting sun. I am the cheated
lover longing

moments between
you and I, my tiny white-hot
tropic sunset deaths.

Hard Candy

Red swirls down
alabaster sink, hungry drain,
peppermint.

Watch it run, skin sacrifice
finger slice, red ribbon,
candy cane.

My only control—drops
blot—heat tattoos sinks' skin,
fireball.

Small universe of self-harm—
bleeding sin for sanity, comfort,
cinnamon.

I do it to feel because I
can't. I can't feel it because I do.
I feel like I can't taste

red flame. Tongue-numb,
hold myself—fiery, fetal,
atomic.

Conjure Music

Break the bones
boil, hollow
hang with twine,
thin as hair,
stagger height
skeleton stairs

bang together, schism maker
baby rattle, fire start.

Polished skull,
agony crown
catching grief
and bloody ripple
razor red,
in slow relief

broken mirror, jackal tooth
necrotic rumor, bled apart.

Canticle pled,
Great Pain,
in deep black
ominous morning,
wet breeze,
afterwind—
Wake.

Volcano bed, serpent tongue,
war drum thunder, broken heart

pagan graveyard
obey in silence
neat and tidy
gift of skin
red-wrapped in ribbons
point of knife.

III

Family Bones

Comfort Remains

Trace a leg fracture
to the early 80s—faulty
ladder, tree cat.

Split a graveyard with a
headache, drop dead suits.
The empty space is screaming.

I'm in bones here, candlelit
window slits dark
unknowable, small plea—come.

Delicate ribs—comb teeth
straighten out these last years,
rearrange your sickness.

One dead night, steady
burn, waxy drip, you came
to tell me you were gone.

But I was dreaming, grainy
film, vintage. Holding your hands
too tightly to hear.

One Way to Get Thin

You missed breakfast—
steamed casket screws,
side of paperwork.

I lunched alone on white
silk, lilac marinade. Where
are you?

Dinner will be boiled
shovel in ground
sauce. Can't blame you

for leaving. We wouldn't
have survived this steady
diet of funerals.

Hardship Hands

Beat up, worn out—calloused
knuckles hump like
graveyard hills.

I tried to shake on a black
exchange—this short robe,
that long soul,

but grief is quicksand and
loss is a sunk cost.

I'll pick up the bones, sort
what is here, what is gone,
what is good for parts.

You are no longer moving forward
in time and if I dress myself—
cool, white, quick—

I can catch up, show you
the stunt and gut of lost life
lines and let it all go.

Psalms

Her hymn was the calm
broadcast, slow

dancing on the same frequency
as nature's wild eye.

Mary blue-eye, a hum to
iron out weathers' wrinkles.

His boomed. Slow beat—
war drums, leading harvests

through dark root and worm.
Compelling sea life to gift.

Hallowed in our child eyes.
The graveyard is fat now,

we recall their songs,
chant them in the family home—

a sacred keep for old gods.

Pushing the Sky

Scotch till I can't and pills—
evening ritual.
Flush, I push off the bed.
I am the sheetrock ceiling, gypsum
tongue.

I nestle in the pink heat of attic
insulation, prickle fluff, I'm tucked,
ready for the permanence
of the grave.

But I'll come slinking down—
hollow ghost, shaky. Sober.
Never have I ever
wanted so much to not recover.

Push harder.
I'm in the trusses, splinter skin,
the black shingles on the roof,
the air itself.

I scatter with blackbirds.
Wet my dried-out poison-tongue
on clouds, I'll long for you,
keep pushing.

Close now, I am darkness,
crowding around your moon—
white light at the
top of night.

At last—ethereal. With you,
I can dissolve as pink hints
of light begin hugging
out the dark.

Quiet Blue Apocalypse

Since terror is a
ladder our senses
sometimes climb, I rise

in deep night and die.
Cryptic,
I know. You know

you didn't give us any
warning? That weird blue,
quiet rising from a

dive, at least warns
of morning. We lost you
in early blue

from black, dark terror,
from black to blue,
ever climbing.

Graveyard Dogs

A full eclipse for
you, scorching beauty.
Tuck away your light—
pocket flame.
Try bringing it out
under stars
know that you can see
what none of us can.
You where you are,
handle ash,
rub your finger
fire out

make us graveyard dogs
nosing stone
unreadable
let us concern
ourselves with smell
your scent burnt out is
enough human for
dogs or granite, marble
or stars.

Casket Obscenity

Finally, weeds are flower-free,
daisy chain. You've moved above
early morning

emergencies, congestion, earthquake
fingertips—hospital visits,
black news, fear.

I'm here, rubbed clean—
kerosene, gunpowder eyes burning
through empty space, bad looks.

Load me up on the wind,
blow my present to its far side.
Lean close, laugh about
caskets and ash.

Let me roll in the comfort
of an unheard voice.
Whisper me again about
the foolishness of bodies.

After

Slit the summer sunrise,
bleed it out over silent horizon.

Sing me songs of youth, nostalgia—
memories too old to doubt.

Dress in storm clouds, flat top—
anvil strike a crooked clock.

Gift me oblivion, silver back,
You long and flashing thing.

Dime-thin, cut in new mouths,
tell me why we aren't talking.

That summer after, I watched
lightning root into earth forever.

I etched bolts into my arms
ribbon flow and curious.

I planted crumbs—
some capacity for personhood so

I could jump off my little
razorblade and back into life.

The Beauty Process

Nightmare year—
black cancer, clots,
and then, unbelievably,

as if the ground
gulped down the sea,
you were gone.

An ocean of liquor,
beaten liver,
I lingered here,

algae eater, bottom
feeder, skin film and
scales.

Unable to keep up
with parts of me
that started playing dead.

But now I am longing for you,
for drying out,

for not becoming the
bog-corpse of a life I
didn't save,

for heating my bones
warm as sunrise, warm as the
other I couldn't.

Resting Easy

The last of your tomatoes
lie obese and red—one
hundred sick Jupiters,
splitting in the sun.

What grows on the broken
backs of withered stems—brown
with rot and diving
after you into the ground,

is a funeral garden.
Your carefully manicured
rows, laid like perfect
plots in a family graveyard.

We lay each other
here, knowing you will till
and toil and father us
for eternity.

Ready to Die

A jagged clock—razorback.
Countless times, thrashing,
was I ready.

With terrible certainty, toothy
wolves, sleek and ruthless—
my road dogs.

Beyond high, plant me in
tombstone patches blooming
between dead

beats of your cancer heart.

Love was not enough,
your rawboned grin came screaming
me awake.

There is no such thing
as an early grave and I was so ready to
die those nights.

Family Bones

Shake a name from your head.
Carve it on a tombstone.

Drop it in the ground,
startle sleep—a waking nightmare.

Shed a mother's tear and
save it in your pocket.

Light a window as a plea,
pray it fit for wandering wind.

Your dark is horror-ripe,
heavy hanging in the next world.

Maybe one dead night, they'll
whisper you awake

to tell you they've gone.
Or that dawn is just a rumor.

So wear a father's grin,
see him in the wrinkles in your skin.

Pin loss firmly on your back.
Roll in family bones.

Sea Legs

for Amiel, all these years later.

Bed sheets spread wide
over living room floor;
the bilge of our boat—
bleached—birds or flowers,
afloat on a soft shag sea.

Down pillows in brown cases,
our slat-wood bulwarks.
Hot chocolate seaman's brew
to help us navigate the night.

In a linen wheelhouse,
the trappings of twilight set
around us, I would sleep under
your weathered arm until I grew
sea legs of my own.

An Acquired Taste

What secret deal
was flame-tongue made—
deep wood, white moon.

Read aloud thrown bones,
and burn into ancient sky.

Nothing's ever ours to keep.

Forest brothers—
fire light, grumble belly,
root in for the long game.

The family plot is tender
suture slice, and gaping.

Favorite color is bleeding.

Overfed, a diet of funerals,
I'll sleep forever to dodge
another tombstone headache.

Because our dead won't stay
pretty long and loss's flavor
is a nightmare.

Tomorrow's Parties

We could small talk a pack
of crayons, reds and

blues—heart valves
trained to dance for you.

Use your favorites, moonflower,
draw me an invitation to leave.

Tonight, I'll fall out of the wind,
sleep it off in the ground,

The best part of aging
is emptying the box, wax nub
paper cut, hand shake.

So, wear your lights, whites,
I'll dig up my dead and
meet you at tomorrow's parties.

Mermaid

After she left, grey man,
you cast a line, longing
for the next world.

I would've sat with you,
still afterglow,
deep loss—forever,

fishing worms, secret ground
moon reverent, stone

petrified at lake's edge,
mountains, trees
ringing our infinite grief.

But the line went,
reason became tidal.
Your eyes lit—a journey set.

I could only watch
as she finally came tugging,
gently reeling you home.

The Turned Corner

You'll be alright.

Depends.

Church wine drunk,
black mass,

nothing good comes
from the ground.

Or the dread of years.

Your cancer stuck
with me.

I hitchhiked on
photograph backs,

living only to give in
to vices, to hide

in the quiet between
terrors, to die.

Grief is cadaver cold,
unconcerned.

It turns out the tether
to whatever is next is
no anchor,

and I feel the current
of night—

air crisp with wishes,
trees dreaming.

I tune in to the
magic in old stones.

So blow out the window
candle.

The moon is enough.

What I needed
came from me,

and nothing hurts
a bit.

Necromance

I admit it. No need
for witches' stone to
sink us.

Save us the gravity of
chest boulders. Your fire

tongues are welcomed.

Because burn as I may, she
is ethereal already and

I will hold the flame—
my evolution to smoke
and ash,

all ascending.

About the Author

Jason Brightwell lives in a tiny town tucked along Maryland's Chesapeake Bay. He holds a B.S. in Forensic Studies and an MFA in Creative Writing—Poetry. His work has been published around the world. He is an avid fan of all things horror as well as movies and music from the 80s and 90s.

You can find him online at www.jasonbrightwell.com and on Instagram @authorjasonbrightwell

Kelsay Books
www.kelsaybooks.com

www.ingramcontent.com/pod-product-compliance
Lightning Source LLC
Chambersburg PA
CBHW021511090426
42739CB00007B/564